10/09

Amazing Animals
Foxes

Please visit our web site at www.garethstevens.com
For a free catalog describing our list of high-quality books, call 1-800-542-2595 (USA) or 1-800-387-3178 (Canada).
Our fax: 1-877-542-2596

Library of Congress Cataloging-in-Publication Data

Barnard, Edward S.
    Foxes / by Edward S. Barnard.
        p. cm. — (Amazing animals)
        Originally published: Pleasantville, NY : Reader's Digest Young Families, c 2007.
        Includes bibliographical references and index.
        ISBN-10: 0-8368-9117-1   ISBN-13: 978-0-8368-9117-1 (lib. bdg.)
        ISBN-10: 1-4339-2121-9   ISBN-13: 978-1-4339-2121-6 (soft cover)
    1. Foxes—Juvenile literature. I. Title.
    QL737.C22B339 2009
    599.775—dc22   2009002329

This edition first published in 2010 by
Gareth Stevens Publishing
A Weekly Reader® Company
1 Reader's Digest Road
Pleasantville, NY 10570-7000 USA

This edition copyright © 2010 by Gareth Stevens, Inc. Original edition copyright © 2007 by Reader's Digest Young Families,
Pleasantville, NY 10570

Executive Managing Editor: Lisa M. Herrington
Senior Editor: Brian Fitzgerald
Senior Designer: Keith Plechaty

Produced by Editorial Directions, Inc.
Art Direction and Page Production: The Design Lab/Kathleen Petelinsek and Gregory Lindholm
Consultant: Robert E. Budliger (Retired), NY State Department of Environmental Conservation

Photo Credits
Front cover: Photodisc/Getty Images; title page: Corel Corporation; contents page: Corel Corporation; pages 6–7: Digital Vision; page 8: Corel Corporation; page 10: Image Source; page 11: Image Source; page 12: Corel Corporation; pages 14–15: Corel Corporation; page 16: Corel Corporation; page 19: Corel Corporation; page 20: Dreamstime.com/Nicola Gavin; page 21: Corel Corporation; pages 22–23: Dynamic Graphics, Inc.; page 24: Dynamic Graphics, Inc.; page 25: Dynamic Graphics, Inc.; page 27: Dynamic Graphics, Inc.; page 28: Corbis Corporation; pages 30–31: Photodisc/Getty Images; page 32 (main): Image Source; page 32 (left inset): iStockphoto.com/Kit Sen Chin; page 32 (right inset): Corel Corporation; page 35: Corel Corporation; page 36 (main): Image Source; page 36 (inset): Digital Vision; page 37: Dynamic Graphics, Inc.; pages 38–39: Corel Corporation; page 41: Corel Corporation; page 43: Corel Corporation; pages 44–45: Image Source; page 46: Corel Corporation; back cover: Corel Corporation.

Printed in the United States of America

1 2 3 4 5 6 7 8 9 14 13 12 11 10 09

Amazing Animals
Foxes

By Edward S. Barnard

Gareth Stevens
Publishing

Contents

Chapter 1
A Fox Story

A red fox is hunting for mice that it can bring to its family in the den.

It is March in the North Woods. A wind is blowing the snow that still covers the forest floor. Underground, a mother red fox is curled up in her **den**. Her bushy tail is wrapped like a blanket around five fluffy, dark gray newborn **kits**. Blind and helpless, each kit weighs only 4 ounces (113 grams) and is about the size of a mouse. Each has a tiny tail tipped with white. The kits snuggle up against their mother's warm belly and drink her milk.

From time to time, the father fox brings his mate something to eat. She gulps it down hungrily. The mother has not been outside to hunt since her kits were born two weeks earlier.

The eyes of the kits are now open. The kits are taking an interest in their brothers and sisters, and they are beginning to explore the den. A thick coat of charcoal gray fur has replaced their baby fluff.

Wild Words

A male fox is called a dog or a **reynard**. A female fox is called a **vixen**. A baby fox is called a kit, a pup, or a cub.

The mother fox begins to leave the den to hunt, but the father still brings her food. She returns often to the kits who quickly cuddle against her to nurse. The mother plays with the kits and grooms them by licking each kit all over.

The kits are growing fast now. Their mother's milk is three times richer than cow's milk. Their tiny **milk teeth** are coming in. The kits chew and suck on meat brought by their parents.

When the kits are a month old, they leave the den for the first time. Their mother stands guard nearby. Once the kits get used to being outside, they explore the area around the entrance to their den. Every day the kits stay outside a little longer.

The hungry kits begin biting and wrestling over food. They pull and tug until one kit gets a piece of meat or the piece is torn in two. The toughest kit usually wins the contest.

When they are about a month old, red fox kits begin changing color from charcoal gray to light tan.

What Do You Call a Fox?

Here are a few of the words for a fox in other languages: *vos* (Dutch), *volpe* (Italian), *lisa* (Russian), *hu* (Chinese), *kitsune* (Japanese), *tsula* (Cherokee), *renard* (French), *zorro* (Spanish), and *roka* (Hungarian).

Still playful, these fox kits are nearly four months old and have red fur like their parents. Soon they will begin hunting on their own.

When the mother and father foxes have food, they call to the kits. The young foxes rush from the den. They squirm on their stomachs and wag their tails. Then one kit runs up to the parent and begs for the food. Nipping and nuzzling around the adult's mouth, this kit usually gets fed first.

In May, the days grow longer. The kits' coats are changing color from gray to light tan. Their eyes are turning from blue to yellow. The mother fox makes it difficult for the kits to nurse by lying on her stomach when they try to drink milk.

By the time the kits are eight weeks old, their permanent teeth have replaced their milk teeth. They are now eating only solid food. By June, the mother and father foxes are bringing food less and less often to the den. Occasionally the parents will take the kits hunting. But most of the time, the young foxes are on their own.

By late June, the kits have grown red coats and are almost as big as their parents. Now they must find food by themselves. By October, some of the males go off to look for a mate. The females stay near the den. Some stay until December. One or two young female foxes may even stay until spring and help their parents raise another family.

Chapter 2
The Body of a Fox

A red fox has a white
tip on its bushy tail.

The Largest Fox

The red fox is the largest of all the foxes. It is about twice the size of a house cat but not as big as a wolf or a coyote. A red fox looks bigger than it really is because of its bushy coat and extra-long, bushy tail. Its tail is called a **brush** or a sweep. The red fox has a sharp nose, large ears, and a long, thin body. Its back legs are longer than the front ones.

Like other foxes, the red fox can pull in its claws partway. The claws stay sharp because they don't always scrape the ground. Foxes walk on their toes and have fur growing around their foot pads. This makes them sure-footed, silent runners.

The red fox is extremely swift on its feet. It can run more than 35 miles (56 kilometers) an hour on flat ground. That's about the speed of a car in the **suburbs**. The red fox can also swim well when it needs to.

A Long Runner

A red fox measures about 26 inches (66 centimeters) from the tip of its nose to the base of its tail. But its tail can measure anywhere from 12 inches (30 cm) to 24 inches (61 cm). So when a red fox runs with its tail straight behind, it can be 4 feet (122 cm) long!

Super Senses

Foxes have long whiskers around their noses and soft hairs near their paws. These help them find **prey** moving in grass or snow. Foxes also have yellow eyes with dark, almond-shaped pupils. Foxes cannot see as clearly as humans do in daylight. However, they can easily detect moving things in semidarkness.

Foxes have very sensitive hearing. Most types of foxes have large ears that are the shape of triangles. Their ears are always twitching to help them figure out where sounds are coming from. Their ears are especially tuned to the noises that small animals make when they are on the move or nibbling on plants.

Foxes "see" with their noses almost as well as we see with our eyes. When they pass through a forest, foxes notice all kinds of smells. They can smell a pinecone, mushroom, berry bush, or chipmunk burrow.

Nosy Foxes

Foxes can smell odors much better than humans can. Foxes have many more odor-detecting glands, or sensors, in their noses than we do—more than 200 million of them.

A red fox has a long, thin snout that is good for searching small holes for food.

A red fox usually has orange-red fur, but it can have a yellow, black, or silver coat.

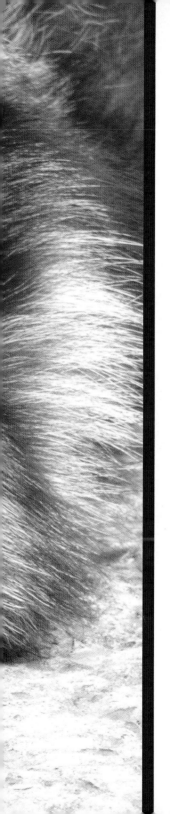

Fox Fur

A red fox usually has orange-red fur that covers most of its head and back. It has white fur under its snout and on its chest, belly, and the tip of its tail. There is black fur on its feet.

Sometimes a kit in a red fox litter will grow up to be a silver fox. During the winter, a silver fox has thousands of long black hairs growing throughout its mostly silver undercoat. Another red fox, called a cross fox, also has a red coat. A black stripe runs along its back to its tail and a black stripe runs over its shoulders. These color combinations can all occur in one litter.

A red fox sheds its fur every year beginning in spring. Then it begins growing a new coat. During this shedding process, called **molting**, the fox's coat looks scruffy. Patches of old fur fall off and new fur grows in. The new coat is complete by late summer or early fall.

Coat Tails

The tail of a red fox is always tipped with white, no matter what color the fox's coat is.

Chapter 3
Fox Families

Fox Trot

A young male red fox is likely to leave home between October and January to look for a mate. If he is in a suburb with lots of garbage, he may travel only a few miles in his search. If he is in the wild where food is harder to find, he may travel 100 miles (161 km) or more.

A fox kit greets a parent by licking and nipping at the corners of the adult's mouth.

Fox Family Life

A red fox hunts alone, but it usually doesn't live alone. Most red foxes are part of a family that includes a male, a female, and kits. The family may also have a "helper" or two. Helpers are female foxes that were born the year before. Instead of leaving the den area, the helpers remain with their parents. They sometimes babysit and bring home food for the kits.

Fall and early winter is a time of change for red fox families. Kits born in the spring are getting old enough to look for mates and form new families. Young males begin fighting with their parents and leave home to seek mates. Some parents may even be pushed out of a den area by their children. The family may also leave the den and move to a different place.

Good Grooming

This gray fox mother, like all fox mothers, grooms her kits to keep them clean. Fox kits also groom one another. Grooming helps family members bond together. Female kits usually receive more grooming than males and tend to stay with their families longer.

Better First Than Last

From the time kits are a week old, they fight over food. After a month, the strongest and most forceful kit has won most of the scuffles. Scientists call this kit the **alpha** kit. The other kits let the alpha kit get food first.

The kits play-fight, but they are rarely violent with one another. Whenever a kit gets some food, it must struggle to keep it. Higher-ranking kits steal food from lower-ranking kits. If there is plenty of food, all the kits survive. But if food is scarce, the lowest-ranking kit may not live to be an adult. This may seem unfair. However, the strongest kits will have the best chance of surviving and producing another family of foxes.

There is also a system among older foxes. The mother is the alpha vixen. She gets first pick of food brought to the den. Helper foxes have to wait for leftovers or find their own food.

Wild Words

The members a fox family organize themselves in order from strongest to weakest. Scientists call this system **dominance order**.

Fox kits spend hours playing near their den. They wait for their parents to return with food.

With his ears held back and tail twisted, a young male red fox runs away from an alpha male. The alpha male doesn't allow other males in his territory.

Whose Paw Print?

Fox paw prints are easy to confuse with those of dogs and cats. One way to tell the difference is to look at the rear pad. The rear pads of dogs and cats look a bit like bicycle seats. The fox's rear pad doesn't.

Large Dog   **Large Cat**   **Fox**

Starting a Family

When a young male red fox leaves his parents in the fall, he also leaves behind the shelter of a family den and familiar surroundings. The days get shorter and the nights longer. This is helpful at first because the young fox hunts mainly at night. However, as the weather turns colder, mice and other small animals are harder to find.

The first snowfall makes life even more difficult. It is no longer easy to smell prey or the **scent** marks left by alpha male foxes. Foxes make these scent marks on trees and bushes to warn other foxes to stay away. When an alpha male meets a younger male fox in his **territory**, the two foxes rear up on their hind legs. They bare their teeth and flatten their ears. They try to knock each other down. Usually the older fox wins.

If he can avoid hunters, coyotes, and alpha males, the young male fox will find an area he wants to settle in. If he meets a young female fox, he might ignore her at first. When she leaves strong-smelling scents on tree trunks, though, he will follow her. Slowly, he will move closer and closer. When the vixen is ready, the pair will mate and begin a family.

Chapter 4
Surviving in the Wild

Using its powerful hind legs, a red fox can leap into the air, sail 15 feet (5 meters) over flat ground, and land with its front paws on its prey!

Lightweight

A red fox weighs 12 to 15 pounds (5 to 7 kilograms). A dog the same size, such as a cocker spaniel, weighs about 25 pounds (11 kg). The red fox's thin bones and small stomach make it light on its feet.

Cocker Spaniel

Red Fox

Jumping for Joy

Red foxes love to pounce on other animals, and they start pouncing when they are very young. They jump playfully on their brothers and sisters. As the red foxes grow up, they pounce on everything they hear or see moving—from crickets and butterflies to birds and mice. Pouncing behavior is part of a fox's nature. Foxes pounce for the fun of it—and to survive.

Hiding Snacks

The red fox cannot eat large meals because it has a small stomach. It can eat only a pound and a half (680 grams) of food at a time. That's about three good-sized hamburgers. A wolf, in comparison, can eat 20 pounds (9 kg) of meat at one meal.

The red fox makes up for its small appetite by storing food it can't eat right away. After catching a mouse, the fox will bury it. Then the fox pushes the dirt back with its nose and rearranges the leaves and twigs to make the place look like it has not been disturbed. The fox usually remembers where it has stored its snack. A few hours or days later, the fox returns, digs up the mouse, and eats it—if another animal hasn't found it already!

Family Den

A red fox needs a large area in which to live. Its territory ranges from the size of one football field to thousands of football fields.

In its territory, a female red fox looks for an empty hole made by another animal that can be enlarged into a fox family den. Fox dens have several entrances so parents and kits can escape from danger quickly. Female foxes have a number of dens in their territory. They move their kits from one den to another to keep them safe.

Foxes have big territories and are active mostly at night. This means they need ways of communicating that don't depend on seeing. To warn other foxes to stay away, foxes mark trees and rocks with their scent. They also mark places where they have dug up food. Such markings tell others that the food is gone.

Local and Long Distance Calls

Red foxes use calls to communicate with one another. A wow-wow barking call is used over long distances. A short cough-like bark warns kits of danger. Kits at play make a low stuttering noise. A female fox makes a spine-tingling howl during mating season to attract males. Male foxes sometimes make this sound, too.

Slopes with sandy, yellow soil are ideal places for red foxes to make their dens. The soil matches the color of young kits.

All Ears

A bat-eared fox's ears are each about 5 inches (13 cm) long. This fox's hearing is so good that it can find insects moving underground!

The tiny fennec fox of Africa is the world's smallest fox. It is 18 inches (46 cm) long and only 8 inches (20 cm) tall. It weighs just 2 to 3 pounds (about 1 kg)!

Some Foxes Like It Hot

The red fox has a number of **habitats**. It lives in forests, marshes, farmlands, and suburbs. Other types of foxes live in hot or cold places. The fennec fox and the bat-eared fox live in African deserts. The feet of the fennec fox are covered with fur. This protects the fox from the broiling-hot desert sand. Its tan coat helps the fox blend in with its sandy habitat so that **predators** won't see it easily. The tan color reflects sunlight, which helps keep the fox cooler. The thick underfur of the fennec fox keeps it warm on cold desert nights.

One Fox Likes It Cold

The Arctic fox is the only fox that lives in the freezing cold of the Far North. Its white fur coat is even warmer than the coat of a polar bear! Its feet are covered with fur. Its short ears and legs help keep the fox warmer by reducing the size of places where body heat can escape. Its tail is so long that the Arctic fox can cover its nose and feet for extra warmth when it curls up. The white fur helps the fox blend into its snowy surroundings and protect it from predators.

Chapter 5
Foxes in the World

Where Red Foxes Live

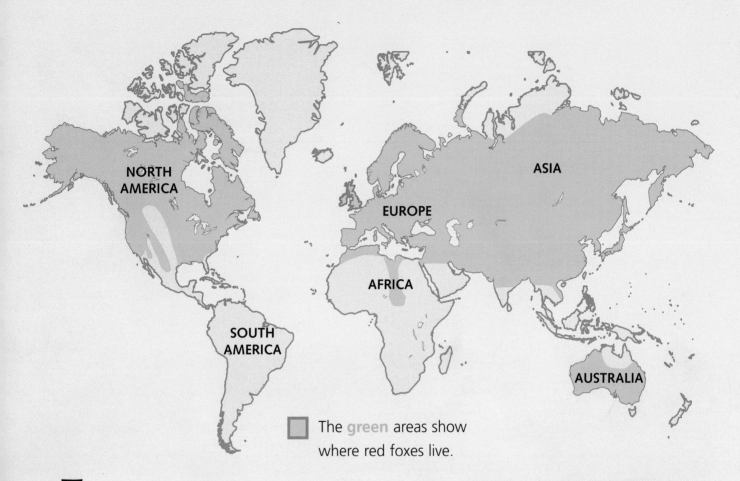

NORTH
AMERICA

ASIA

EUROPE

AFRICA

SOUTH
AMERICA

AUSTRALIA

The green areas show
where red foxes live.

Foxes live on every continent around the globe except Antarctica. The red fox has the largest **range**. It lives on five of the continents. It is a native of North America, parts of Africa, Asia, and Europe. European settlers brought the red fox to Australia. Red foxes live at the edges of forests, in marshes, and on farmlands. They also make their homes in suburbs where people live.

On Six Continents

Foxes are members of the dog family, which scientists call *Canidae*. The *Canidae* family includes foxes, dogs, wolves, jackals, and coyotes. There are more than 25 **species** of foxes around the world, and they can be found on six continents.

The red fox lives in more places than any other kind of fox. One reason it can survive in so many different places is that the red fox is **omnivorous** (om-NIV-ur-uhss). This means it eats both plants and animals.

In fact, the red fox eats almost any food it finds! In wild areas, it eats small mammals such as rats, voles, mice, squirrels, and rabbits. It also eats birds, earthworms, insects, dead fish, crabs, fruits, and even grass. In areas where people live, the red fox raids garbage cans and dumps.

A Breed Apart

Although coyotes, dogs, and wolves mate with each other, foxes do not mate with any other members of the *Canidae* family. Foxes are related to dogs and wolves, but can seem more similar to cats. They split off from other *Canidae* groups about 12 million years ago.

Foxes and People

Red foxes can live up to about 15 years in **captivity**. They rarely survive more than three or four years in the wild. Diseases and predators, such as dogs, kill many red foxes. But humans are the biggest threat. They hunt foxes for sport and kill them for fur.

Many farmers consider red foxes to be pests because they kill chickens. However, foxes also eat large numbers of mice and rabbits. This helps reduce farmers' crop losses and control diseases carried by mice. Foxes play an important role in the web of life.

Fast Facts About Red Foxes

Scientific name	*Vulpes vulpes*
Class	Mammals
Order	Carnivora
Size	Height: 13–15 inches (33–38 cm)
	Body length: about 26 inches (66 cm)
	Tail length: 12–24 inches (30–61 cm)
Weight	12–15 pounds (5–7 kg)
Life span	About 3–4 years in the wild
	About 15 years in captivity
Habitat	Forests, marshes, farmlands, suburbs
Top speed	About 35 miles (56 km) per hour

The red fox is intelligent and crafty. It has managed to survive in places where many other wild animals have died out.

Glossary

alpha—the leader of a group

brush—a fox's bushy tail

captivity—a confined space, such as a zoo

den—a place where an animal raises its young and rests

dominance order—a system in which some animals have a higher rank than others

habitat—the natural environment where a plant or animal lives

kit—a young fox

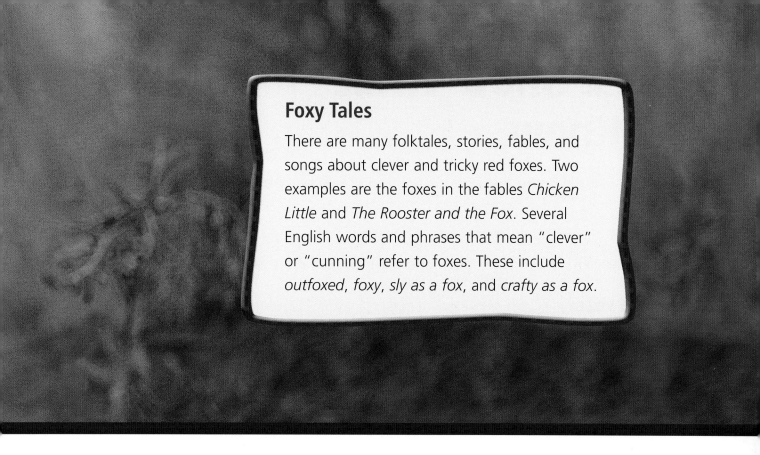

Foxy Tales

There are many folktales, stories, fables, and songs about clever and tricky red foxes. Two examples are the foxes in the fables *Chicken Little* and *The Rooster and the Fox*. Several English words and phrases that mean "clever" or "cunning" refer to foxes. These include *outfoxed*, *foxy*, *sly as a fox*, and *crafty as a fox*.

milk teeth—teeth of a young mammal that fall out and are replaced by permanent teeth

molting—shedding old fur, hair, or skin and having new grow in

omnivorous—eating plants and meat

predator—an animal that hunts and eats other animals to survive

prey—animals that are hunted by other animals for food

range—all the places where a species lives

reynard—a male fox

scent—a smell left by an animal that other animals can identify

species—a group of living things that are the same in many ways

suburbs—neighborhoods outside a big city

territory—an area that an animal considers to be its own and will fight to defend

vixen—a female fox

Foxes: Show What You Know

How much have you learned about foxes? Grab a piece of paper and a pencil and write your answers down.

1. How old are kits when their permanent teeth replace their milk teeth?

2. What is a vixen?

3. How fast can a red fox run?

4. How many odor-detecting glands do foxes have in their noses?

5. What happens to a fox's fur every spring?

6. How do mother foxes keep their kits clean?

7. Why does the snow make life difficult for foxes?

8. How much food can a fox eat at one time?

9. Red foxes live on which five continents?

10. Which type of fox is the smallest?

1. Eight weeks old 2. TA female fox 3. More than 35 miles (56 km) per hour 4. More than 200 million 5. It sheds and gets replaced by new fur. 6. By grooming them with their tongues 7. It makes it harder to smell prey and scent marks. 8. A pound and a half (680 g) 9. North America, Europe, Asia, Australia, and Africa 10. The fennec fox

For More Information

Books

Lockwood, Sophie. *Foxes* (The World of Mammals). Mankato, MN: The Child's World, 2008.

Murphy, Patricia J. *Red Foxes* (Grassland Animals). Mankato: MN: Capstone Press, 2006.

Stuhr, Carri. *Arctic Foxes* (Early Bird Nature Books). Minneapolis: Lerner Publications, 2009.

Web Sites

Animal Planet

http://animal.discovery.com/mammals/fox

Learn new facts, watch videos, and find out about wild dogs that are related to the fox.

National Geographic: Red Fox

http://animals.nationalgeographic.com/animals/mammals/red-fox.html

Check out this site for fun facts, photos, and videos of foxes in the wild.

Publisher's note to educators and parents: Our editors have carefully reviewed these web sites to ensure that they are suitable for children. Many web sites change frequently, however, and we cannot guarantee that a site's future contents will continue to meet our high standards of quality and educational value. Be advised that children should be closely supervised whenever they access the Internet.

Index